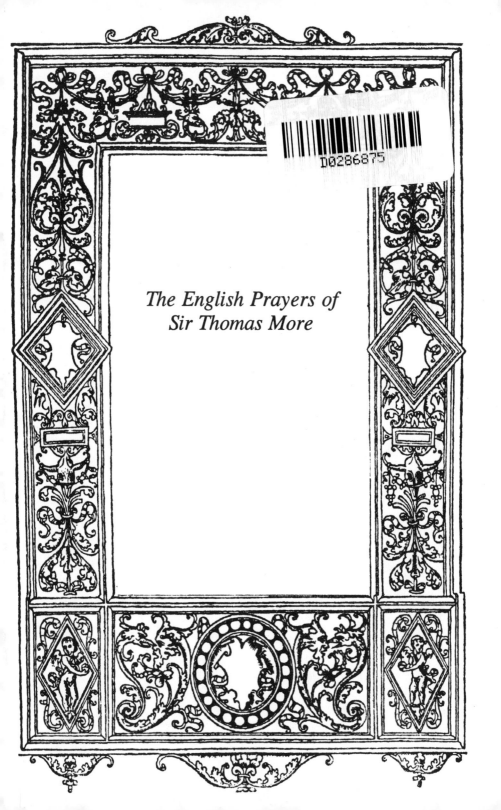

*The English Prayers of
Sir Thomas More*

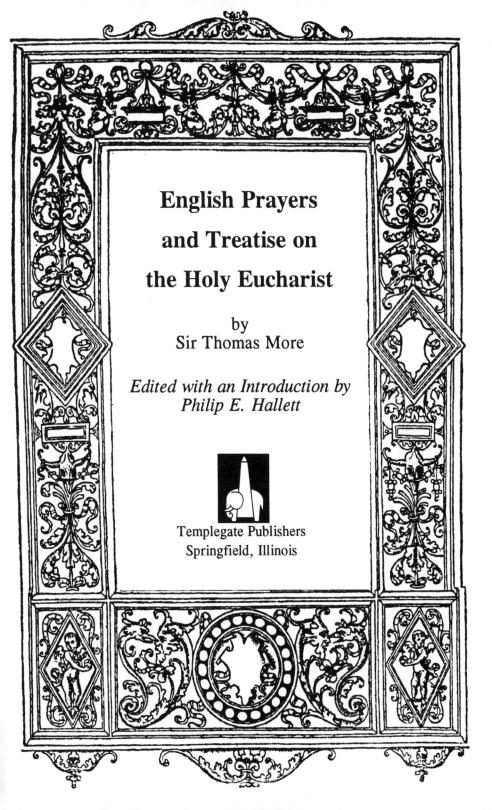

# English Prayers
# and Treatise on
# the Holy Eucharist

by
Sir Thomas More

*Edited with an Introduction by*
*Philip E. Hallett*

Templegate Publishers
Springfield, Illinois

© 1995 Templegate Publishers

Templegate Publishers
302 East Adams Street
P.O. Box 5152
Springfield, Illinois 62705

ISBN 0-87243-137-1

Library of Congress Catalog Card Number 95-60059

# The Contents

# The Introduction

**T**he pieces here reprinted are all taken from the volume of St Thomas More's English Works which William Rastell, the saint's nephew, edited in 1557.

The earliest prayer in time is from a Latin original and concludes St Thomas's little group of translations connected with John Picus, Earl of Mirandula. When the future martyr came to the conclusion that he was called, not to the cloister, but to life in the world, he sought for a holy and learned layman whom he might put before his eyes as a model, and fixed upon the famous humanist Pico. From this fact and other indications it is probable that the translations were made in or about the year 1505, the year of his marriage.[1]

The prayer is a pleasing example of More's verses. We have placed in brackets syllables which, though not according to modern usage, must be sounded if the rhythm is not to suffer.

All the other pieces of this volume were written during the saint's imprisonment in the Tower from April 1534 until his death. Such at least is Rastell's testimony.

Until his books and papers were all removed, he worked away busily. Besides many smaller works he wrote the lengthy *Dialogue of Comfort* and the equally lengthy, though unfin-

ished, *Treatise upon the Passion.*
Most of the latter work the saint wrote
in English, and the parts that he left
in Latin were translated by Mistress
Mary Basset, the daughter of Margaret Roper, printed and placed after
St Thomas More's work by Rastell.
At the end of each section of the
saint's own English work comes a
prayer. These prayers we have here
printed under headings which indicate
the nature of the respective sections to
which they form the conclusion. Both
in form and matter they are admira-
ble. Much has been written recently
of Cranmer's gift for English devo-
tional prose. In balance, simplicity,
and tenderness of feeling, some of
these prayers (take, for example, the
one headed 'Christ Foretells His Passion') will fully sustain comparison

with his. Perhaps we should add that Rastell is none too accurate a printer, and it is likely that here and there slight emendations would improve the text.

The well-known 'Godly Meditation' still exists in the saint's own handwriting upon the margin of his Book of Hours, now in the possession of the Earl of Denbigh. Perhaps it is from this circumstance or perhaps it is from internal evidence that some have surmised that it was written when he resigned the Chancellorship, two years before his imprisonment. This is not supported, however, by Rastell's introductory note.

We know that one of the saint's favourite works of devotion was 'The Following of Christ,' which he as-

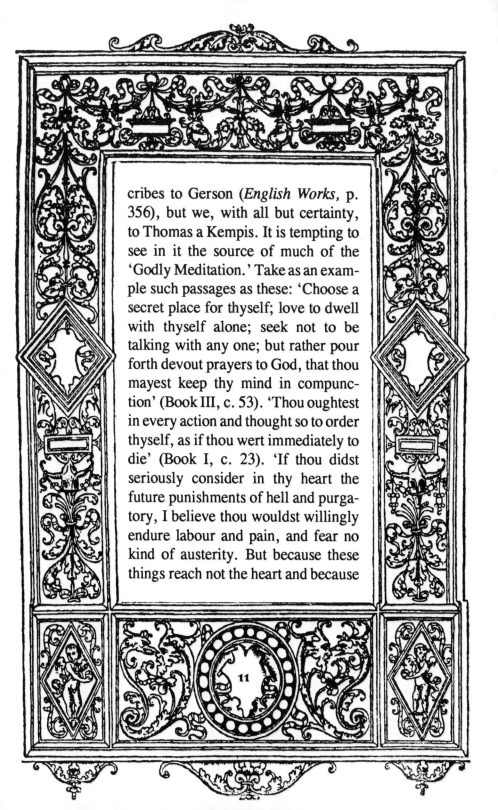

cribes to Gerson (*English Works,* p. 356), but we, with all but certainty, to Thomas a Kempis. It is tempting to see in it the source of much of the 'Godly Meditation.' Take as an example such passages as these: 'Choose a secret place for thyself; love to dwell with thyself alone; seek not to be talking with any one; but rather pour forth devout prayers to God, that thou mayest keep thy mind in compunction' (Book III, c. 53). 'Thou oughtest in every action and thought so to order thyself, as if thou wert immediately to die' (Book I, c. 23). 'If thou didst seriously consider in thy heart the future punishments of hell and purgatory, I believe thou wouldst willingly endure labour and pain, and fear no kind of austerity. But because these things reach not the heart and because

we still love the things that flatter us, therefore we remain cold and very sluggish' (Book I, c. 21). 'The true patient man mindeth not by whom it is he is exercised, whether by ... a good and holy man or by one that is perverse and unworthy, but how much soever and how often soever any adversity happens to him from any thing created, he taketh it all equally from the hand of God with thanksgiving, and esteemeth it a great gain' (Book III, c. 19. Cf. the conclusion of St Thomas's prayer).

Many other passages might be quoted, but as the saint read them in Latin and is here writing in English, it is difficult to trace direct connection, and it may be that the similarities are merely the commonplaces of all ascetic writers.

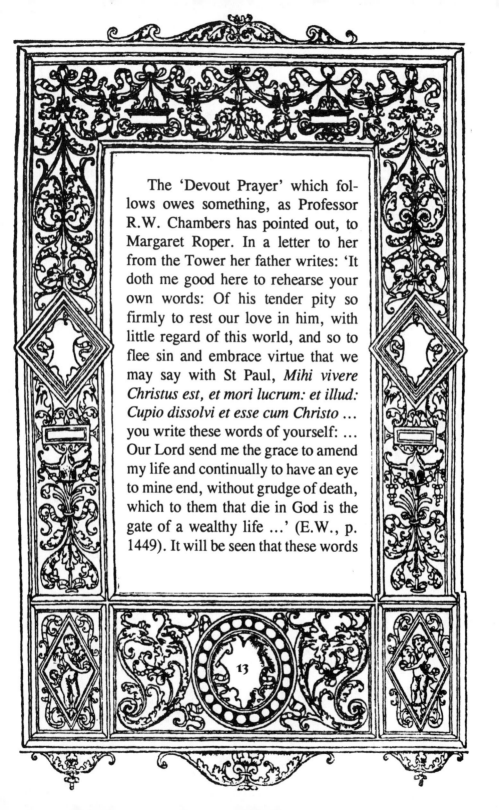

The 'Devout Prayer' which follows owes something, as Professor R.W. Chambers has pointed out, to Margaret Roper. In a letter to her from the Tower her father writes: 'It doth me good here to rehearse your own words: Of his tender pity so firmly to rest our love in him, with little regard of this world, and so to flee sin and embrace virtue that we may say with St Paul, *Mihi vivere Christus est, et mori lucrum: et illud: Cupio dissolvi et esse cum Christo* … you write these words of yourself: … Our Lord send me the grace to amend my life and continually to have an eye to mine end, without grudge of death, which to them that die in God is the gate of a wealthy life …' (E.W., p. 1449). It will be seen that these words

13

are incorporated in St Thomas's prayer.

These are all the formal English prayers that are found in the volume of the English Works, though several of his treatises end in short petitions, such as that God may bring heretics back to the truth, etc. There is, however, a long selection of Latin Psalms and verses from Psalms which is found in the English as well as the Latin works. We have not here transcribed it.

Of the Treatise on the Holy Eucharist we need say little. It will exemplify the saint's hatred of heresy and tender personal love to our Lord. Here, as throughout, we have modernized the spelling and occasionally, where advisable, modified the punctuation. In one instance only have we

14

altered the language: we have repeated the phrase the saint used in connection with the cleansing of the Baptist in his mother's womb, and not used a variant that to modern ears would sound crude. From 1557 until now the treatise has never been reprinted.

May these specimens of his writings increase devotion to St Thomas More, and help to hasten the day when all the rich treasures of his works may be made available in a worthy modern edition.

Philip E. Hallett
Wonersh, 1938.

1. '*The Life of Picus* was printed by More's brother-in-law, John Rastell, and pirated by Wynkyn de Worde. Neither edition bears any date. Much later John Rastell's son, William, dated the translation about 1510; but this is probably the time when his father printed the book, and we may follow the family tradition that it was written about five years earlier.' — R.W. Chambers, *Thomas More*, p. 94.

# A Godly Meditation

*Written by Sir Thomas More, Knight,
while he was a prisoner in the Tower
of London, in the year of our Lord,
1534.*

Give me thy grace, good Lord, To set the world at nought, To set my mind fast upon thee. And not to hang upon the blast of men's mouths. To be content to be solitary, Not to long for worldly company,

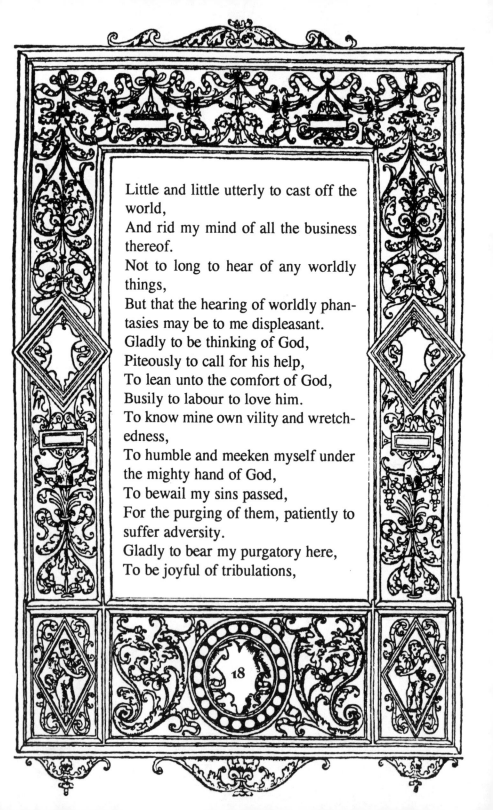

Little and little utterly to cast off the world,
And rid my mind of all the business thereof.
Not to long to hear of any worldly things,
But that the hearing of worldly phantasies may be to me displeasant.
Gladly to be thinking of God,
Piteously to call for his help,
To lean unto the comfort of God,
Busily to labour to love him.
To know mine own vility and wretchedness,
To humble and meeken myself under the mighty hand of God,
To bewail my sins passed,
For the purging of them, patiently to suffer adversity.
Gladly to bear my purgatory here,
To be joyful of tribulations,

18

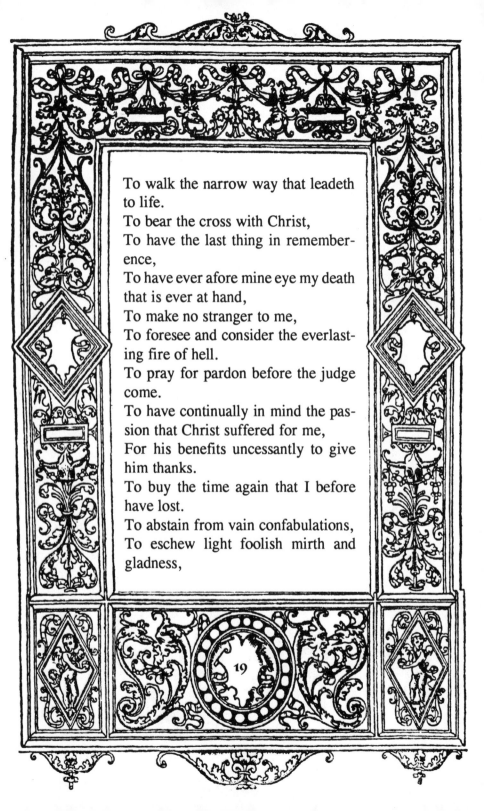

To walk the narrow way that leadeth
to life.
To bear the cross with Christ,
To have the last thing in remember-
ence,
To have ever afore mine eye my death
that is ever at hand,
To make no stranger to me,
To foresee and consider the everlast-
ing fire of hell.
To pray for pardon before the judge
come.
To have continually in mind the pas-
sion that Christ suffered for me,
For his benefits uncessantly to give
him thanks.
To buy the time again that I before
have lost.
To abstain from vain confabulations,
To eschew light foolish mirth and
gladness,

19

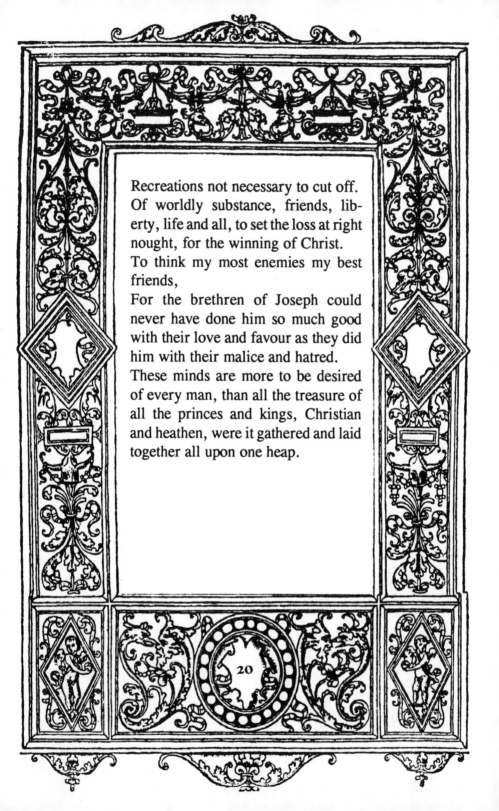

Recreations not necessary to cut off.
Of worldly substance, friends, liberty, life and all, to set the loss at right nought, for the winning of Christ.
To think my most enemies my best friends,
For the brethren of Joseph could never have done him so much good with their love and favour as they did him with their malice and hatred.
These minds are more to be desired of every man, than all the treasure of all the princes and kings, Christian and heathen, were it gathered and laid together all upon one heap.

# A Devout Prayer

*Made by Sir Thomas More, Knight, after he was condemned to die and before he was put to death, who was condemned the Thursday the first day of July in the year of our Lord 1535 and in the 27th year of the reign of King Henry VIII, and was beheaded at the Tower Hill at London, the Tuesday following*

21

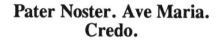

## Pater Noster. Ave Maria. Credo.

**O** Holy Trinity, the Father, the Son, and the Holy Ghost, three equal and co-eternal Persons, and one Almighty God, have mercy on me, vile, abject, abominable, sinful wretch: meekly knowledging before thine High Majesty my long-continued sinful life, even from my very childhood hitherto.

In my childhood, in this point and that point, etc. After my childhood in this point and that point, and so forth by every age, etc.

Now, good gracious Lord, as thou givest me thy grace to knowledge them, so give me thy grace, not in

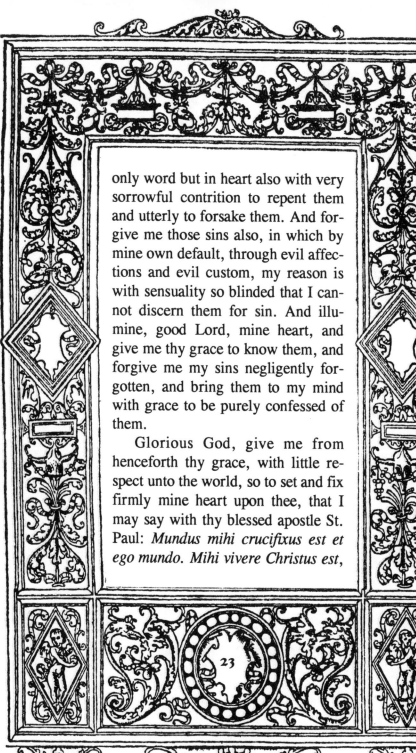

only word but in heart also with very sorrowful contrition to repent them and utterly to forsake them. And forgive me those sins also, in which by mine own default, through evil affections and evil custom, my reason is with sensuality so blinded that I cannot discern them for sin. And illumine, good Lord, mine heart, and give me thy grace to know them, and forgive me my sins negligently forgotten, and bring them to my mind with grace to be purely confessed of them.

Glorious God, give me from henceforth thy grace, with little respect unto the world, so to set and fix firmly mine heart upon thee, that I may say with thy blessed apostle St. Paul: *Mundus mihi crucifixus est et ego mundo. Mihi vivere Christus est, et mori lucrum. Cupio dissolvi et esse cum Christo.*[1]

Give me thy grace to amend my life, and to have an eye to mine end without grudge of death, which to them that die in thee, good Lord, is the gate of a wealthy life.

Almighty God, *Doce me facere voluntatem tuam. Fac me currere in odore unguentorum tuorum. Apprehende manum meam dexteram, et deduc me in via recta propter inimicos meos. Trahe me post te. In chamo et freno maxillas meas constringe, quum non approximo ad te.*[2]

O glorious God, all sinful fear, all sinful sorrow and pensiveness, all sinful hope, all sinful mirth, and gladness take from me. And on the other side concerning such fear, such sorrow, such heaviness, such comfort, consolation and gladness as shall be profitable for my soul: *Fac mecum secundum magnam bonitatem tuam Domine.*[3]

Good Lord, give me the grace, in all my fear and agony, to have recourse to that great fear and wonderful agony that thou, my sweet Saviour, hadst at the Mount of Olivet before thy most bitter passion, and in the meditation thereof, to conceive ghostly comfort and consolation profitable for my soul.

Almighty God, take from me all vain-glorious minds, all appetites of mine own praise, all envy, covetise, gluttony, sloth, and lechery, all wrathful affections, all appetite of revenging, all desire or delight of other folks' harm, all pleasure in provoking any person to wrath and anger, all delight of exprobation or insultation against any person in their affliction and calamity.

And give me, good Lord, an humble, lowly, quiet, peaceable, patient, charitable, kind, tender, and pitiful mind, with all my works, and all my words, and all my thoughts, to have a taste of thy holy, blessed Spirit.

Give me, good Lord, a full faith, a firm hope, and a fervent charity, a love to the good Lord incomparable above the love to myself; and that I love nothing to thy displeasure, but everything in an order to thee.

Give me, good Lord, a longing to be with thee, not for the avoiding of the calamities of this wretched world, nor so much for the avoiding of the pains of purgatory, nor the pains of hell neither, nor so much for the at-

taining of the joys of heaven, in respect of mine own commodity, as even for a very love to thee.

And bear me, good Lord, thy love and favour, which thing my love to thee-ward (were it never so great) could not but of thy great goodness deserve.

And pardon me, good Lord, that I am so bold to ask so high petitions, being so vile a sinful wretch, and so unworthy to attain the lowest. But yet, good Lord, such they be, as I am bounden to wish and should be nearer the effectual desire of them, if my manifold sins were not the let.[4] From which, O glorious Trinity, vouchsafe of thy goodness to wash me, with that blessed blood that issued out of thy tender body, O sweet Saviour Christ, in the divers torments of thy most bitter passion.

Take from me, good Lord, this lukewarm fashion, or rather key-cold manner of meditation and this dullness in praying unto thee. And give me warmth, delight and quickness in thinking upon thee. And give me thy grace to long for thine holy sacraments, and specially to rejoice in the presence of thy very blessed body, sweet Saviour Christ, in the holy sacrament of the altar, and duly to thank thee for thy gracious visitation therewith, and at that high memorial, with tender compassion, to remember and consider thy most bitter passion.

Make us all, good Lord, virtually participant [5] of that holy sacrament this day, and every day make us all lively members, sweet Saviour

Christ, of thine holy mystical body, thy Catholic Church.

*Dignare, Domine, die isto sine peccato nos custodire. Miserere nostri, Domine, miserere nostri.*

*Fiat misericordia tua, Domine, super nos quemadmodum speravimus in te.*

*In te, Domine, speravi, non confundar in aeternum.* [6]

*V. Ora pro nobis, sancta Dei Genitrix.*

*R. Ut digni efficiamur promissionibus Christi.* [7]

## Pro Amicis[8]

Almighty God, have mercy on N. and N. *(with special meditation and consideration of every friend, as godly affection and occasion requireth)*

## Pro Inimicis[9]

Almighty God, have mercy on N. and N., and on all that bear me evil will, and would me harm, and their faults and mine together, by such easy, tender, merciful means, as thine infinite wisdom best can devise,

vouchsafe to amend and redress, and make us saved souls in heaven together where we may ever live and love together with thee and thy blessed saints. O glorious Trinity, for the bitter passion of our sweet Saviour Christ. Amen.

Lord, give me patience in tribulation and grace in everything to conform my will to thine: that I may truly say: *Fiat voluntas tua, sicut in coelo et in terra.* [10]

The things, good Lord, that I pray for, give me thy grace to labour for. Amen.

# A Prayer of Picus Mirandula unto God

O holy God of dreadful majesty, Verily one in three and three in one, Whom angels serve, whose work all creatures be,
Which heaven and earth directest all alone,
We thee beseech, good Lord, with woeful moan

33

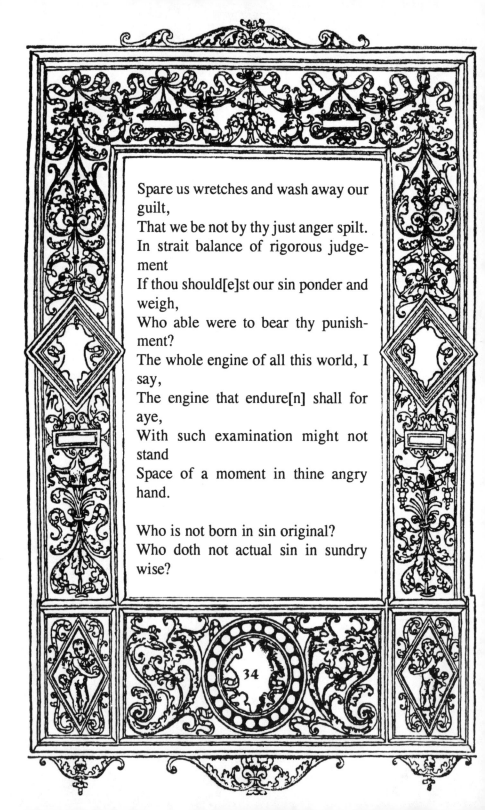

Spare us wretches and wash away our guilt,

That we be not by thy just anger spilt.

In strait balance of rigorous judgement

If thou should[e]st our sin ponder and weigh,

Who able were to bear thy punishment?

The whole engine of all this world, I say,

The engine that endure[n] shall for aye,

With such examination might not stand

Space of a moment in thine angry hand.

Who is not born in sin original?

Who doth not actual sin in sundry wise?

34

But thou, good Lord, art he that spareth all,
With piteous mercy tempering justice.
For as thou dost reward[e]s us devise
Above our merit, so dost thou dispense
The punishment far under our offence.

More is thy mercy far than all our sin.
To give them also that unworthy be[11]
More godly is, and more mercy therein.
Howbeit, worthy enough are they, pardee,[12]
Be they ne'er so unworthy, whom that he
List to accept, which[13] wheresoe'er he taketh

Whom he unworthy findeth worthy
maketh.

Wherefore, good Lord, that aye mer-
ciful art,
Unto thy grace and sov'reign dignity
We silly [14] wretches cry with humble
heart.
Our sins forget and our malignity,
With piteous eyes of thy benignity
Friendly look on us once; thine own
we be
Servants or sinners whether [15] it liketh
thee.

Sinners, if thou our crime behold,
certain,
Our crime the work of our uncour-
teous mind:
But if thy gift[e]s thou behold again,

36

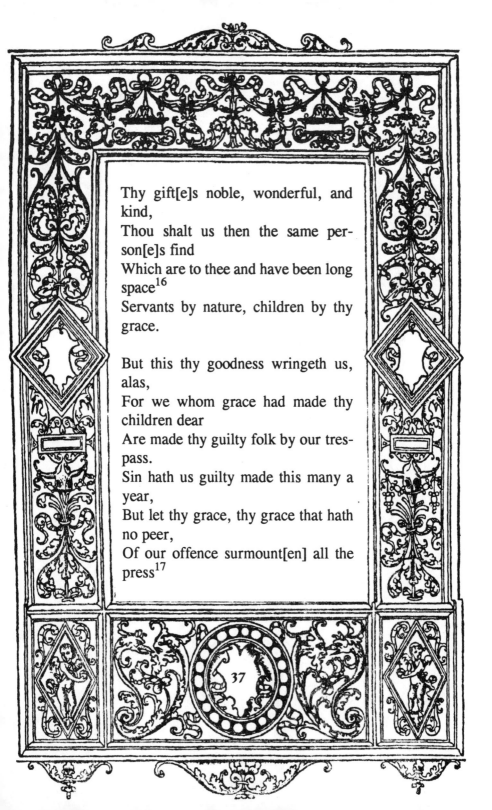

Thy gift[e]s noble, wonderful, and kind,
Thou shalt us then the same person[e]s find
Which are to thee and have been long space[16]
Servants by nature, children by thy grace.

But this thy goodness wringeth us, alas,
For we whom grace had made thy children dear
Are made thy guilty folk by our trespass.
Sin hath us guilty made this many a year,
But let thy grace, thy grace that hath no peer,
Of our offence surmount[en] all the press[17]

That in our time thine honour may increase.
For though thy wisdom, though thy sovereign power,
May otherwise appear sufficiently,
As thing[e]s which thy creatures every hour
All with one voice declare and testify,
Thy goodness yet, thy singular mercy,
Thy piteous heart, thy gracious indulgence
Nothing so clearly show'th as our offence.
What but our sin hath showed that mighty love
Which able was thy dreadful majesty
To draw down into earth from heav'n above,
And cruc'fy God that we poor wretches we

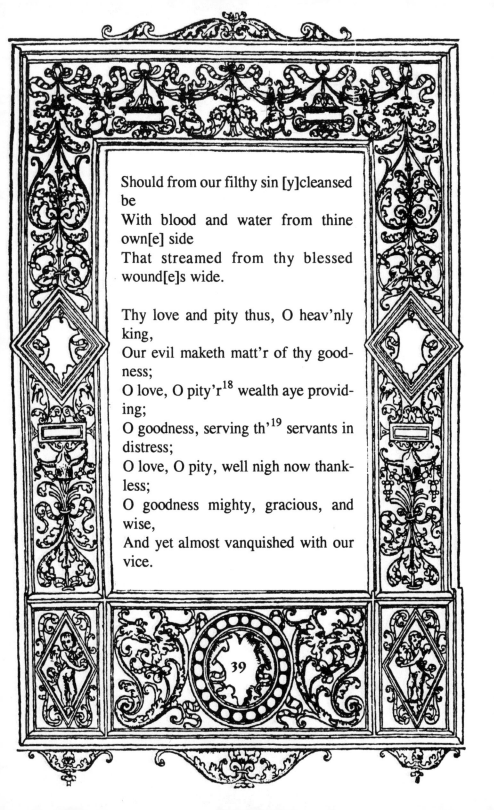

Should from our filthy sin [y]cleansed
be
With blood and water from thine
own[e] side
That streamed from thy blessed
wound[e]s wide.

Thy love and pity thus, O heav'nly
king,
Our evil maketh matt'r of thy goodness;
O love, O pity'r[18] wealth aye provid-
ing;
O goodness, serving th'[19] servants in
distress;
O love, O pity, well nigh now thank-
less;
O goodness mighty, gracious, and
wise,
And yet almost vanquished with our
vice.

Grant, I thee pray, such heat into mine heart,
That to this love of thine may be egal.[20]
Grant me from Satan's service to [a]start
With whom me ru'th so long to have been thrall
Grant me, good Lord and Creator of all
The flame to quench of all sinful desire,
And in thy love set all mine heart afire.

That when the journey of this deadly life
My silly[21] ghost hath finished, and thence
Depart[en] must, without his fleshly wife,

Alone into his lord[es] high presence
He may thee find, O well of indul-
gence,
In thy lordship not as a lord but rather,
As a very tender loving father.
Amen.

# Prayers from the Treatise on the Passion

## The Fall of the Angels

O Glorious blessed Trinity, whose justice hath damned unto perpetual pain many proud rebellious angels, whom thy goodness had created to be partners of thine eternal glory, for thy tender mercy plant in mine heart such meekness that I so may by thy grace follow the motion of my good angel, and so resist the proud suggestions of those spiteful spirits[22] that fell, as I may, through the merits of thy bitter passion, by partner of thy bliss with those holy spirits[22] that stood and now, confirmed by thy grace, in glory shall stand for ever.

### The Fall of Man

Almighty God, that of thine infinite goodness didst create our first parents in the state of innocence, with present wealth and hope of heaven to come, till through the devil's train[23] their folly fell by sin to wretchedness, for thy tender pity of that passion that was paid of their and our redemption, assist me so with thy gracious help, that unto the subtle suggestions of the serpent I never so incline the ears of mine heart but that my reason may resist them and master my sensuality and refrain me from them.

## The Decree of Man's Redemption

O Holy blessed Saviour Jesus Christ, which willingly didst determine to die for man's sake, mollify mine hard heart and supple it so by grace, that through tender compas-

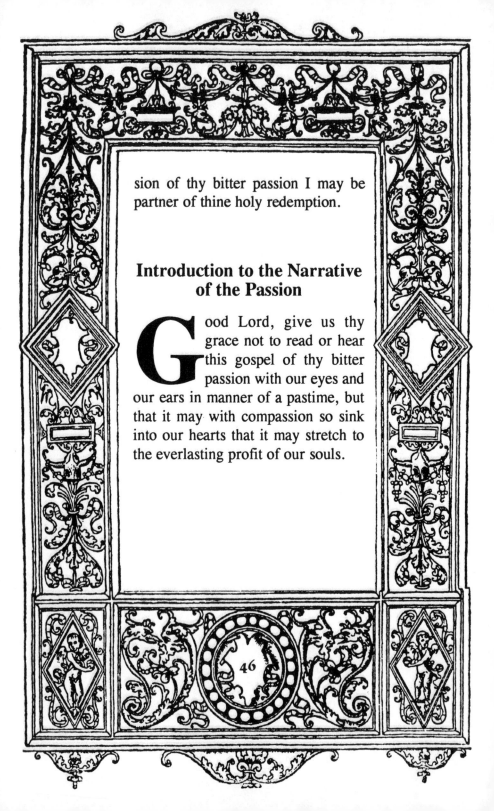

sion of thy bitter passion I may be partner of thine holy redemption.

## Introduction to the Narrative of the Passion

Good Lord, give us thy grace not to read or hear this gospel of thy bitter passion with our eyes and our ears in manner of a pastime, but that it may with compassion so sink into our hearts that it may stretch to the everlasting profit of our souls.

### The Paschal Supper

Good Lord, which upon the sacrifice of the paschal lamb didst so clearly destroy the first-begotten children of the Egyptians, that Pharao was thereby forced to let the children of Israel depart out of his bondage, I beseech thee give me the grace in such faithful wise to receive the very sweet paschal lamb, the very blessed body of our sweet Saviour thy son, that, the first suggestions of sin by thy power killed in my heart, I may safe depart out of the danger of the most cruel Pharao the devil.

## Christig Foretells His Passion

Good Lord, give me the grace so to spend my life, that when the day of my death shall come, though I feel pain in my body, I may feel comfort in soul; and with the faithful hope of thy mercy, in due love towards thee and charity towards the world, I may, through thy grace, part hence into thy glory.

## The Priests and Ancients Conspire Against Christ

Gracious God, give me thy grace so to consider the punishment of that false great council that gathered together against thee, that I be never, to thy displeasure, partner nor give mine assent to follow the sinful device of any wicked counsel.

## The Treason of Judas

O My sweet Saviour Christ, whom thine own wicked disciple, entangled with the devil through vile wretched covetise betrayed, inspire, I beseech thee, the marvel of thy majesty with the love of thy goodness, so deep into mine heart, that in respect of the least point of thy pleasure, my mind may set always this whole wretched world at nought.

### 'He Loved Them Unto the End'

O My sweet Saviour Christ, which (in) thine undeserved love towards mankind, so kindly wouldst suffer the painful death of the cross, suffer not me to be cold nor lukewarm in love again towards thee.

## The Disciples Find a Room
## For the Last Supper

Almighty Jesus Christ, which wouldst for our example observe the law that thou camest to change, and being maker of the whole earth wouldst have yet no dwelling-house therein, give us thy grace so to keep thine holy law, and so to reckon ourselves for no dwellers but for pilgrims upon earth, that we may long and make haste, walking with faith in the way of virtuous works, to come to the glorious country wherein thou hast bought us inheritance for ever with thine own precious blood.

## The Washing of the Feet

Almighty Jesus, my sweet Saviour Christ, which wouldst vouchsafe thine own almighty hands to wash the feet of thy twelve apostles, not only of the good but of the very traitor too, vouchsafe, good Lord, of thine excellent goodness, in such wise to wash the foul feet of mine affections, that I never have such pride enter into mine heart as to disdain either in friend or foe, with meekness and charity for the love of thee, to file[24] mine hands with washing of their feet.

## Institution of the Holy Eucharist

**O**ur most dear Saviour Christ, which after the finishing of the old paschal sacrifice hast instituted the new sacrament of thine own blessed body and blood for a memorial of thy bitter passion, give us such true faith therein, and such fervent devotion thereto, that our souls may take fruitful ghostly food thereby.

# A Treatise

*To Receive the Blessed Body of Our Lord Sacramentally and Virtually Both, Made in the Year of Our Lord 1534, by Sir Thomas More, Knight, While He Was Prisoner in the Tower of London, Which He Entitled Thus as Followeth: To Receive the Blessed Body of Our Lord Sacramentally and Virtually Both*

They receive the blessed body of our Lord both sacramentally and virtually, which in due manner and worthily receive the blessed sacrament. When I say worthily, I mean not that any man is so good, or can be so good, that his goodness could make him, of very right and reason, worthy to receive into his vile earthly body that holy blessed glorious flesh and blood of Almighty God himself, with his celestial soul therein and with the majesty of his eternal godhead; but that he may prepare himself, working with the grace of God, to stand in such a state as the incomparable goodness of God will, of his liberal bounty, vouchsafe to take and accept for worthy to receive his own inestimable

precious body into the body of so simple a servant.

Such is the wonderful bounty of Almighty God that he not only doth vouchsafe, but also doth delight, to be with men, if they prepare to receive him with honest and clean souls, whereof he saith: *Deliciae meae esse cum filiis hominum.* My delight and pleasures are to be with the sons of men.[25]

And how can we doubt that God delighteth to be with the sons of men, when the Son of God and very Almighty God himself liked not only to become the son of man, that is to wit, the son of Adam the first man, but over that in his innocent manhood to suffer his painful passion for the redemption and restitution of man.

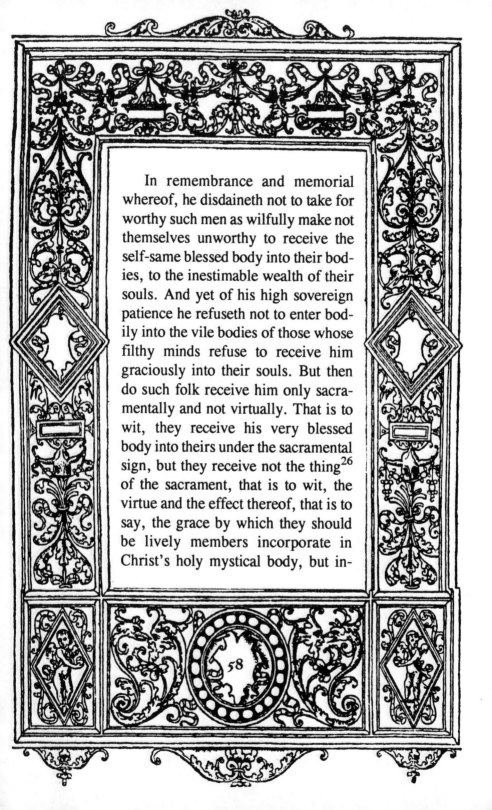

In remembrance and memorial whereof, he disdaineth not to take for worthy such men as wilfully make not themselves unworthy to receive the self-same blessed body into their bodies, to the inestimable wealth of their souls. And yet of his high sovereign patience he refuseth not to enter bodily into the vile bodies of those whose filthy minds refuse to receive him graciously into their souls. But then do such folk receive him only sacramentally and not virtually. That is to wit, they receive his very blessed body into theirs under the sacramental sign, but they receive not the thing[26] of the sacrament, that is to wit, the virtue and the effect thereof, that is to say, the grace by which they should be lively members incorporate in Christ's holy mystical body, but in-

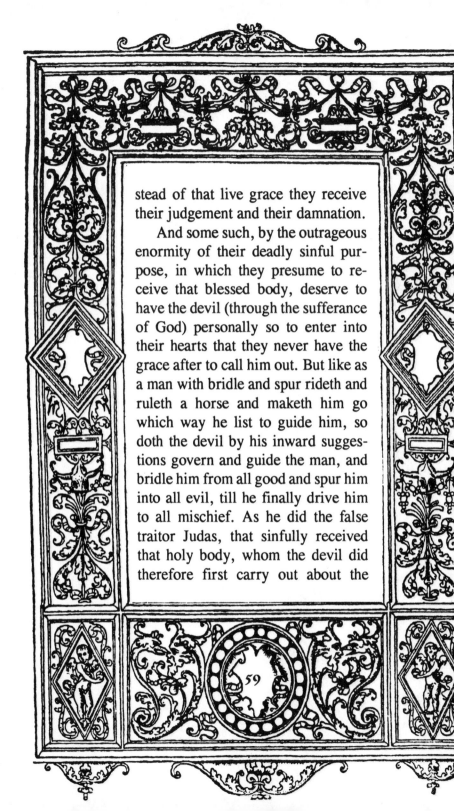

stead of that live grace they receive their judgement and their damnation.

And some such, by the outrageous enormity of their deadly sinful purpose, in which they presume to receive that blessed body, deserve to have the devil (through the sufferance of God) personally so to enter into their hearts that they never have the grace after to call him out. But like as a man with bridle and spur rideth and ruleth a horse and maketh him go which way he list to guide him, so doth the devil by his inward suggestions govern and guide the man, and bridle him from all good and spur him into all evil, till he finally drive him to all mischief. As he did the false traitor Judas, that sinfully received that holy body, whom the devil did therefore first carry out about the traitorous death of the self-same blessed body of his most loving master, which he so late so sinfully received, and within a few hours after unto the desperate destruction of himself.

And therefore have we great cause with great dread and reverence to consider well the state of our own soul, when we shall go to the board of God, and as near as we can (with the help of his special grace diligently prayed for before) purge and cleanse our souls by confession, contrition and penance, with full purpose of forsaking from henceforth the proud desires of the devil, the greedy covetise[27] of wretched worldly wealth, and the foul affection of the filthy flesh, and be in full mind to persevere and continue in the ways of God and holy

cleanness of spirit: lest that if we presume so unreverently to receive this precious margarite, this pure pearl, the blessed body of our Saviour himself contained in the sacramental sign of bread, that like a sort of swine, rooting[28] in the dirt and wallowing in the mire, we tread it under the filthy feet of our foul affections, while we set more by them than by it, intending to walk and wallow in the puddle of foul filthy sin, therewith the legion of devils may get leave of Christ so to enter into us, as they got leave of him to enter into the hogs of Genesareth; and as they ran forth with them, and never stinted till they drowned them in the sea, so run on with us (but if God of his great mercy refrain them and give us the grace to repent), else not fail to drown us in the deep sea of everlasting sorrow.

Of this great outrageous peril the blessed apostle St Paul giveth us gracious warning, where he saith in his first epistle to the Corinthians: *Quicunque manducaverit panem et biberit calicem Domini indigne, reus erit corporis et sanguinis Domini:* Whosoever eat the body and drink the cup of our Lord unworthily, he shall be guilty of the body and blood of our Lord.[29]

Here is, good christian readers, a dreadful and terrible sentence, that God here, by the mouth of his holy apostle, giveth against all them that unworthily receive this most blessed sacrament, that their part shall be with Pilate and the Jews, and with that false traitor Judas; since God reputeth the unworthy receiving and eating of his blessed body for a like heinous offence against his majesty as he accounted theirs that wrongfully and cruelly killed him.

And therefore to the intent that we may avoid well this importable [30] danger, and in such wise receive the body and blood of our Lord as God may of his goodness accept us for worthy, and therefore not only enter with his blessed flesh and blood sacramentally and bodily into our bodies, but also with his Holy Spirit graciously and effectually into our souls, Saint Paul, in the place afore remembered, saith: *Probet seipsum homo, et sic de pane illo edat, et de calice bibat:* Let a man prove himself, and so eat of that bread and drink of that cup. But then in what wise shall we

prove ourselves? We may not go rashly to God's board, but by a convenient time taken before. We must, as I began to say, consider well and examine surely what state our soul standeth in.

In which thing it will be not only right hard, but also peradventure impossible, by any possible diligence of ourselves, to attain unto the very full undoubted surety thereof, without special revelation of God. For, as the scripture saith: *Nemo vivens scit, utrum odio vel amore dignus sit:* No man living knoweth whether he be worthy the favour or hatred of God.[31] And in another place: *Etiamsi simplex fuero, hoc ipsum ignorabit anima mea:* If I be simple, that is to say, without sin, that shall not my mind surely know.[32]

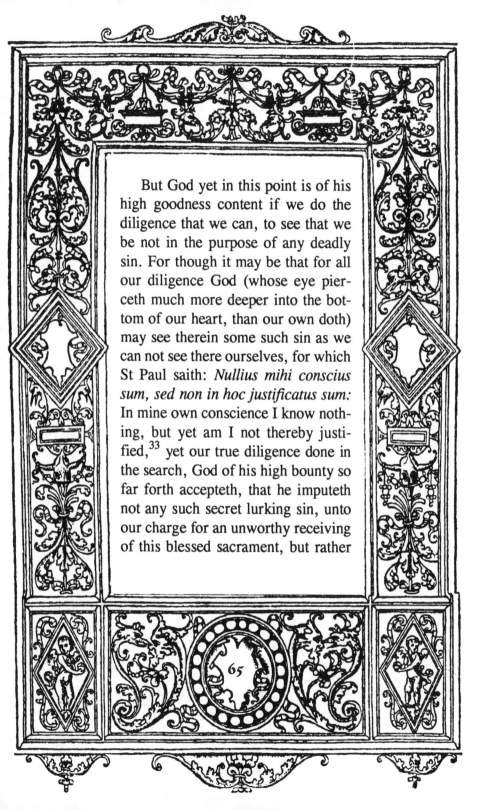

But God yet in this point is of his high goodness content if we do the diligence that we can, to see that we be not in the purpose of any deadly sin. For though it may be that for all our diligence God (whose eye pierceth much more deeper into the bottom of our heart, than our own doth) may see therein some such sin as we can not see there ourselves, for which St Paul saith: *Nullius mihi conscius sum, sed non in hoc justificatus sum:* In mine own conscience I know nothing, but yet am I not thereby justified,[33] yet our true diligence done in the search, God of his high bounty so far forth accepteth, that he imputeth not any such secret lurking sin, unto our charge for an unworthy receiving of this blessed sacrament, but rather

the strength and virtue thereof pur-
geth and cleanseth that sin.[34]

In this proving and examination of
ourself, which St Paul speaketh of,
one very special point must be to
prove and examine ourself and see
that we be in the right faith and belief
concerning the holy blessed sacrament itself. That is to wit, we verily
believe that it is, as indeed it is, under
the form and likeness of bread, the
very blessed body, flesh, and blood of
our holy Saviour Christ himself, the
very same body, and the very self
same blood, that died and was shed
upon the cross for our sin, and the
third day gloriously did arise again to
life and, with the souls of holy saints
fetched out of hell, ascended and
stied[35] up wonderfully into heaven
and there sitteth on the right hand of

the father, and shall visibly descend in great glory to judge the quick and the dead, and reward all men of their works.

We must, I say, see that we firmly believe that this blessed sacrament is not a bare sign or a figure or a token of that holy body of Christ, but that it is, in perpetual remembrance of his bitter passion that he suffered for us, the self same precious body of Christ that suffered it, by his own almighty power and unspeakable goodness consecrated and given to us.

And this point of belief is, in the receiving of this blessed sacrament, of such necessity and such weight, with them that have years and discretion, that without it they receive it plainly to their damnation. And that point believed very full and fastly must needs be a great occasion to move any man in all other points to receive it well. For note well the words of St Paul therein: *Qui manducat de hoc pane et bibit de calice indigne, judicium sibi manducat et bibit, non dijudicans corpus domini:* He that eateth of this bread and drinketh of this cup unworthily, eateth and drinketh judgement upon himself in that he discerneth not the body of our Lord.

Lo! Here this blessed apostle well declareth that he which in any wise unworthily receiveth this most excellent sacrament receiveth it unto his own damnation, in that he well declareth by his evil demeanour towards it, in his unworthy receiving of it, that he discerneth it not, nor judgeth it, nor taketh it for the very body of our Lord, as in deed it is.

68

And verily it is hard but that this point, deeply rooted in our breast, should set all our heart in a fervour of devotion, towards the worthy receiving of that blessed body.

For surely there can be no doubt on the other side, but that if any man believe that it is Christ's very body, and yet is not inflamed to receive him devoutly thereby, that man were likely to receive this blessed sacrament very coldly and far from all devotion, if he believed that it were not his body, but only a bare token of him instead of his body.

But now having the full faith of this point fastly grounded in our heart, that the thing which we receive is the very blessed body of Christ, I trust there shall not greatly need any great information farther to teach us, or any

great exhortation farther to stir and excite us, with all humble manner and reverant behaviour to receive him.

For if we will but consider, if there were a great worldly prince which for special favour that he bare us would come visit us in our own house, what a business we would then make, and what a work it would be for us, to see that our house were trimmed up in every point, to the best of our possible power, and everything so provided and ordered, that he should by his honourable receiving perceive what affection we bear him, and in what high estimation we have him; we should soon by the comparing of that worldly prince and this heavenly prince together (between which twain is far less comparison than is between a man and a mouse) inform and teach ourself with how lowly mind, how tender loving heart, how reverent humble manner we should endeavor ourself to receive this glorious heavenly king, the king of all kings, almighty God himself, that so lovingly doth vouchsafe to enter, not only into our house (to which the noble man Centurio acknowledged himself unworthy) but his precious body into our vile wretched carcase, and his holy spirit into our poor simple soul.

What diligence can here suffice us? What solicitude can we think here enough against the coming of this almighty king, coming for so special gracious favour, not to put us to cost, not to spend of ours, but to enrich us of his, and that after so manifold deadly displeasures done him so unkindly by us, against so many of his incomparable benefits before done unto us. How would we now labour and foresee that the house of our soul (which God were coming to rest in) should neither have any poisoned spider or cobweb or deadly sin hanging in the roof, nor so much as a straw or a feather of any light lewd thought that we might spy in the floor, but we would sweep it away.

But forasmuch, good Christian reader, as we neither can attain this great point of faith nor any other virtue but by the special grace of God, of whose high goodness every good thing cometh (for as St James saith: *Omne datum optimum et omne donum perfectum desursum est, descendens a patre luminum:* Every good gift and every perfect gift is from above, descending from the father of lights[36])

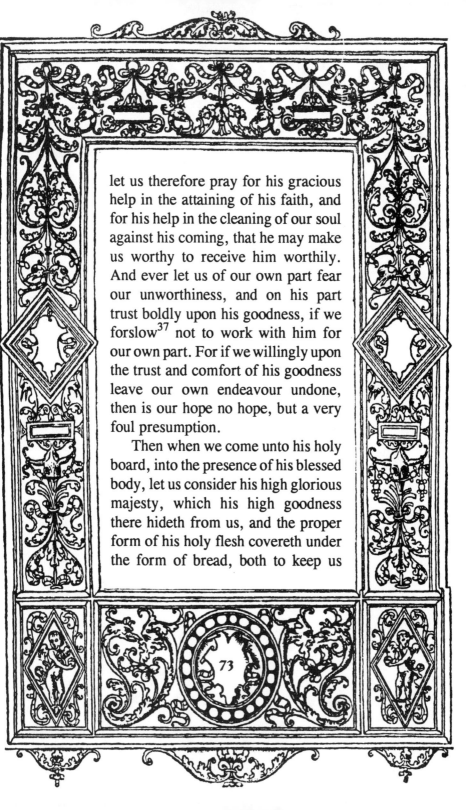

let us therefore pray for his gracious help in the attaining of his faith, and for his help in the cleaning of our soul against his coming, that he may make us worthy to receive him worthily. And ever let us of our own part fear our unworthiness, and on his part trust boldly upon his goodness, if we forslow[37] not to work with him for our own part. For if we willingly upon the trust and comfort of his goodness leave our own endeavour undone, then is our hope no hope, but a very foul presumption.

Then when we come unto his holy board, into the presence of his blessed body, let us consider his high glorious majesty, which his high goodness there hideth from us, and the proper form of his holy flesh covereth under the form of bread, both to keep us

from abashment such as we could not peradventure abide, if we (such as we yet be) should see and receive him in his own form such as he is, and also for the increase of the merit of our faith in the obedient belief of that thing at his commandment, whereof our eyes and our reason seem to show us the contrary.

And yet forasmuch as although we believe it, yet is there, in many of us that believe, very faint and far from the point of such vigour and strength as would God it had, let us say unto him with the father that had the dumb son: *Credo, domine, adjuva incredulitatem meam:* I believe, Lord, but help thou my lack of belief:[38] and with his blessed apostles: *Domine, adauge nobis fidem:* Lord, increase faith in us.[39] Let us also with the poor publican, in knowledge of our own unworthiness, say with all meekness of heart: *Deus propitius esto mihi peccatori:* Lord God, be merciful to me, sinner that I am.[40] And with the Centurio: *Domine, non sum dignus ut intres sub tectum meum:* Lord, I am not worthy that thou shouldst come into my house.[41]

And yet with all this remembrance of our own unworthiness and therefore the great reverence, fear and dread for our own part, let us not forget on the other side to consider his inestimable goodness, which disdaineth not, for all our unworthiness, to come unto us and to be received of us.

But likewise as at the sight of receiving this excellent memorial of his death (for in the remembrance thereof doth he thus consecrate and give his own blessed flesh and blood unto us) we must with tender compassion, remember and call to mind the bitter pains of his most painful passion. And yet therewithal rejoice and be glad in the consideration of his incomparable kindness, which in his so suffering for us, to our inestimable benefit he showed and declared towards us. So must we be both sore afeard of our own unworthiness, and yet therewith be right glad and in great hope at the consideration of his unmeasurable goodness.

St Elizabeth, at the visitation and salutation of our blessed Lady, having by revelation the sure inward knowledge that our Lady was conceived with our Lord, albeit that she was herself such as else for the diversity between their ages she well might and would have thought it but convenient and meetly that her young cousin should come visit her, yet now because she was mother to our Lord, she was sore amarvelled of her visitation and thought herself far unworthy thereto; and therefore said unto her: *Unde hoc, ut veniat mater Domini mei ad me?* Whereof is this, that the mother of our Lord should come to me?[42] But ye for all the abashment of her own unworthiness she conceived thoroughly such a glad blessed comfort, that her holy child St John the Baptist leapt in her womb for joy: Whereof she said: *Ut facta est vox salutationis tuae in auribus meis, exultavit gaudio infans in utero meo:* As soon as the voice of thy salutation was

in mine ears, the infant in my womb leapt for joy.

Now like as St Elizabeth by the spirit of God had those holy affections, both of reverent considering her own unworthiness in the visitation of the mother of God, and yet for all that so great inward gladness therewith, let us at this great high visitation, in which not the mother of God, as came to St Elizabeth, but one incomparably more excelling the mother of God than the mother of God passed St Elizabeth, doth so vouchsafe to come and visit each of us with his most blessed presence, that he cometh not into our house but into our self, let us, I say, call for the help of the same holy spirit that then inspired her, and pray him at this high and holy visitation so to inspire us, that we may both be abashed with the reverent dread of our own unworthiness, and yet therewith conceive a joyful consolation and comfort in the consideration of God's inestimable goodness. And that each of us, like as we may well say with great reverent dread and admiration: *Unde hoc, ut veniat Dominus meus ad me?* Whereof is this, that my Lord should come unto me? (and not only unto me but also into me), so we may with glad heart truly say at the sight of his blessed presence: *Exultavit gaudio infans in utero meo:* The child in my womb, that is to wit, the soul in my body, that should be then such a child in innocence, as was that innocent infant St John, leapeth, good Lord, for joy.

Now when we have received our Lord and have him in our body, let us

not then let him alone, and get us forth about other things and look no more unto him (for little good could he, that so would serve any guest) but let all our business be about him. Let us by devout prayer talk to him, by devout meditation talk with him. Let us say with the prophet: *Audiam quid loquatur in me Dominus:* I will hear what our Lord will speak within me. [43]

For surely if we set aside all other things and attend unto him, he will not fail with good inspirations to speak such things to us within us as shall serve to the great spiritual comfort and profit of our soul. And therefore let us with Martha provide that all our outward business may be pertaining to him, in making cheer to him and to his company for his sake; that is to wit, to poor folk of which he taketh every one, not only for his disciple, but also as for himself. For himself saith: *Quamdiu fecistis uni de his fratribus meis minimis, mihi fecistis:* That that you have done to one of the least of these my brethren, you have done it to myself.[44]

And let us with Mary also sit in devout meditation and harken well what our Saviour, being now our guest, will inwardly say unto us. Now have we a special time of prayer, while he that hath made us, he that hath bought us, he whom we have offended, he that shall judge us, he that shall either damn us or save us, is of his great goodness become our guest and is personally present within us, and that for no other purpose but to be sued unto for pardon and so thereby to save us.

Let us not lose this time therefore, suffer not this occasion to slip, which we can little tell whether ever we shall get it again or never. Let us endeavour ourself to keep him still, and let us say with his two disciples that were going to the castle of Emmaus: *Mane nobiscum, Domine:* Tarry with us, good Lord:[45] and then shall we be sure that he will not go from us, but if we unkindly put him from us. Let us not play [? pray] like the people of Genesareth, which prayed him to depart out of their quarters, because they lost their hogs by him, when instead of the hogs he saved the man, out of whom he cast the legion of devils that after destroyed the hogs. Let not us likewise rather put God from us by unlawful love of worldly winning, or foul filthy lust, rather than for the

profit of our soul to forbear it. For sure may we be that when we wax such, God will not tarry with us, but we put him unkindly from us.

Nor let us not do as did the people of Jerusalem, which on Palm Sunday received Christ royally and full devoutly with procession, and on the Friday after put him to a shameful passion. On the Sunday cried: *Benedictus qui venit in nomine Domini:* Blessed be he that cometh in the name of our Lord:[46] and on the Friday cried out: *Non hunc sed Barabbam:* We will not have him but Barabbas.[47] On the Sunday cried: *Hosanna in excelsis;* on the Friday: *Tolle, tolle, crucifige eum.*[48] Sure if we receive him never so well, nor never so devoutly at Easter, yet whensoever we fall after to such wretched sinful liv-

ing, as casteth our Lord in such wise out of our souls, as his grace tarrieth not with us, we show ourself to have received him in such manner as those Jews did. For we do as much as in us is, to crucify Christ again: *Iterum* (saith St Paul) *crucifigentes filium Dei*.[49]

Let us, good Christian readers, receive him in such wise as did the good publican Zaccheus, which when he longed to see Christ, and because he was but low of stature, did climb up into a tree. Our Lord seeing his devotion called unto him and said: Zaccheus, come off and come down, for this day must I dwell with thee. And he made haste and came down, and very gladly received him into his house. But not only received him with a joy of a light and soon sliding affec-

84

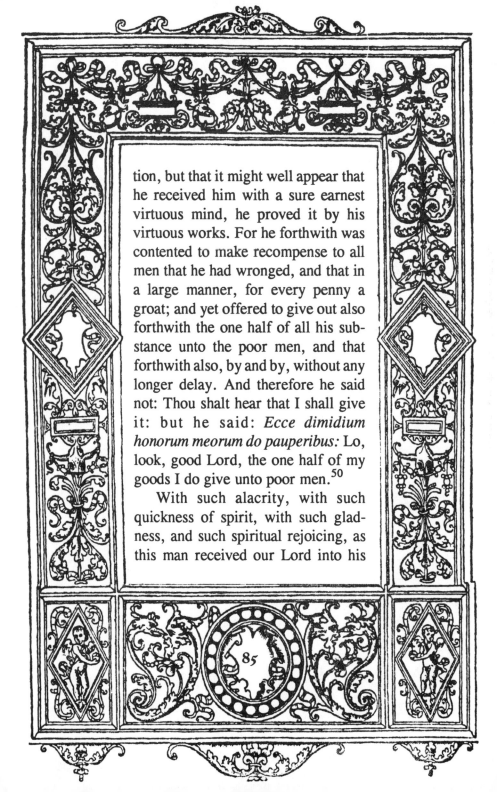

tion, but that it might well appear that
he received him with a sure earnest
virtuous mind, he proved it by his
virtuous works. For he forthwith was
contented to make recompense to all
men that he had wronged, and that in
a large manner, for every penny a
groat; and yet offered to give out also
forthwith the one half of all his substance unto the poor men, and that
forthwith also, by and by, without any
longer delay. And therefore he said
not: Thou shalt hear that I shall give
it: but he said: *Ecce dimidium
honorum meorum do pauperibus:* Lo,
look, good Lord, the one half of my
goods I do give unto poor men.[50]

With such alacrity, with such
quickness of spirit, with such gladness, and such spiritual rejoicing, as
this man received our Lord into his

house, our Lord give us the grace to receive his blessed body and blood, his holy soul, and his almighty godhead, both into our bodies and into our souls, that the fruit of our good works may bear witness unto our conscience that we receive him worthily and in such a full faith, and such a stable purpose of good living, as we be bounden to do. And then shall God give a gracious sentence and say upon our soul, as he said upon Zaccheus: *Hodie salus facta est huic domui:* This day is health and salvation come unto this house: which that holy blessed person of Christ, which we verily in the blessed sacrament receive, through the merit of his bitter passion (whereof he hath ordained his only blessed body, in that blessed sacrament, to be the memorial) vouchsafe,

good Christian readers, to grant unto
us all.

# Footnotes

1. 'The world is crucified to me and I to the world' (Gal. 6.14). 'To me to live is Christ, and to die is gain' (Phil. 1.21). 'I desire to be dissolved and to be with Christ' (ibid. 23).

2. 'Teach me to do thy will' (Ps. 142.10). 'Make me to run after thee to the odour of thy ointments' (Cant. 1.3). 'Take thou my right hand and guide me in the straight path because of my enemies' (Passages from the Psalms). 'Draw me after thee' (Cant. 1. 3). 'With bit and bridle bind fast

my jaws when I come not near unto thee' (Ps. 31.9).

3. 'Deal with me according to thy great goodness, O Lord' (cf. Ps. 118.124).

4. hindrance.

5. sharers in the virtue.

6. 'Deign, O Lord, to keep us on that day without sin. Have mercy on us, O Lord, have mercy on us. Let thy mercy, O Lord, be upon us, as we have hoped in thee. In thee, O Lord, have I hoped, let me not be confounded for ever' (*From the* 'Te Deum').

7. 'Pray for us, O holy mother of God. That we may be made worthy of the promises of Christ.'

8. For my friends.

9. For my enemies.

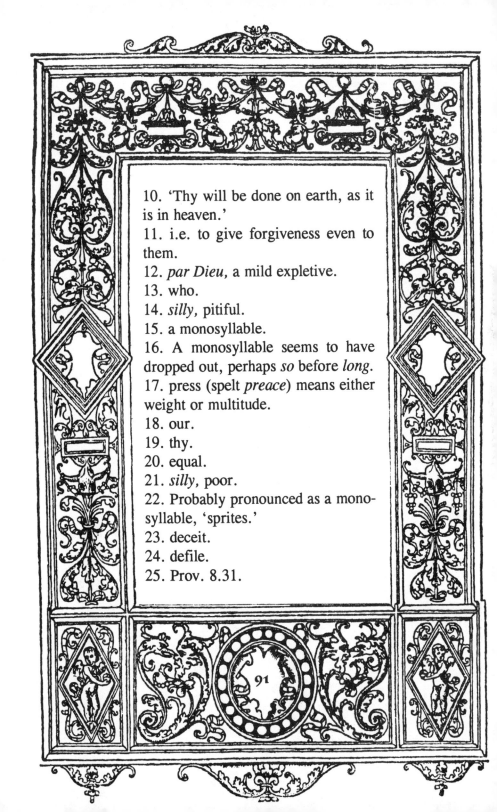

10. 'Thy will be done on earth, as it is in heaven.'

11. i.e. to give forgiveness even to them.

12. *par Dieu,* a mild expletive.

13. who.

14. *silly,* pitiful.

15. a monosyllable.

16. A monosyllable seems to have dropped out, perhaps *so* before *long*.

17. press (spelt *preace*) means either weight or multitude.

18. our.

19. thy.

20. equal.

21. *silly,* poor.

22. Probably pronounced as a monosyllable, 'sprites.'

23. deceit.

24. defile.

25. Prov. 8.31.

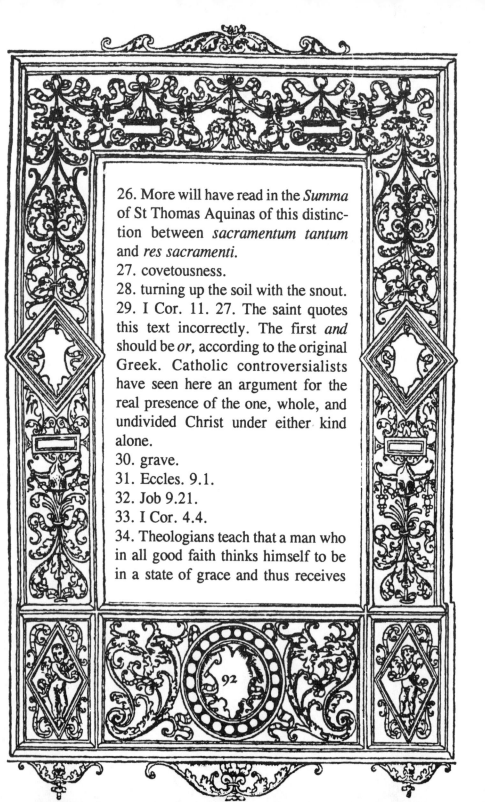

26. More will have read in the *Summa* of St Thomas Aquinas of this distinction between *sacramentum tantum* and *res sacramenti.*

27. covetousness.

28. turning up the soil with the snout.

29. I Cor. 11. 27. The saint quotes this text incorrectly. The first *and* should be *or,* according to the original Greek. Catholic controversialists have seen here an argument for the real presence of the one, whole, and undivided Christ under either kind alone.

30. grave.

31. Eccles. 9.1.

32. Job 9.21.

33. I Cor. 4.4.

34. Theologians teach that a man who in all good faith thinks himself to be in a state of grace and thus receives

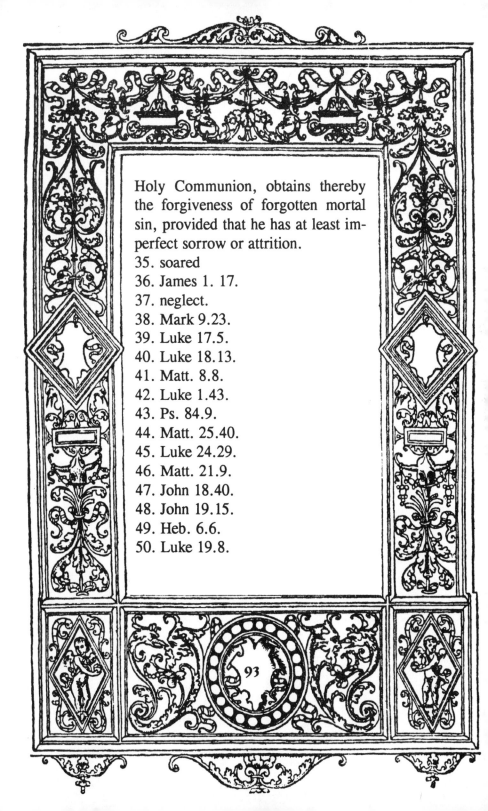

Holy Communion, obtains thereby the forgiveness of forgotten mortal sin, provided that he has at least imperfect sorrow or attrition.

35. soared
36. James 1. 17.
37. neglect.
38. Mark 9.23.
39. Luke 17.5.
40. Luke 18.13.
41. Matt. 8.8.
42. Luke 1.43.
43. Ps. 84.9.
44. Matt. 25.40.
45. Luke 24.29.
46. Matt. 21.9.
47. John 18.40.
48. John 19.15.
49. Heb. 6.6.
50. Luke 19.8.

# Chronology

Thomas More was born in London on February 7, 1478, the son of John More, a barrister, later a judge, and Agnes Graunger. At the age of 13 he was placed in the household of Cardinal Morton, Archbishop of Canterbury and Lord Chancellor. He entered Canterbury Hall, Oxford (subsequently absorbed by Christ Church) about 1492. After a two year residence he was recalled to London and entered New Inn as a law student. In 1496 he was admitted to Lincoln's Inn and the following year met Erasmus who became his lifelong friend. He was elected a member of Parliament in 1504 and the following year he married Jane, daughter of John Colt of Newhall, Essex. They had four children – Margaret, Elizabeth, Cecilia and John. Jane More died in 1511 and More later married a widow, Alice Middleton. In 1510 More was made Under-Sheriff of London. More was with Henry VIII at the "Field of the Cloth of Gold" in June 1520. Knighted in 1521, he was made sub-treasurer to the king and in 1523 became Speaker of the House of Commons on Wolsey's recommendation. In 1529 More succeeded Wolsey as Lord Chancellor of England. The Act of Succession was passed in March, 1534 and the month following More was sent to the Tower of London as a prisoner. He was beheaded on July 6, 1535 on Tower Hill.